Borderline Personality Disorder

Signs, Symptoms, and Treatment for Emotional Insecurity

Charles Tillman

Table of Contents

Introduction

Patients with borderline personality disorder (BPD) are famous for being difficult. Their problems can challenge even the most experienced therapists.

The most frightening symptoms of BPD are chronic suicidal ideation, repeated suicide attempts, and self-mutilation. These are the patients we worry about—and are afraid of losing. After a difficult session, therapists may not be sure if they will ever see the patient again or whether someone will telephone to report a suicide.

Even in patients not threatening suicide, therapists face serious difficulties. BPD is associated with many symptoms, and each one presents problems. Mood instability is difficult to manage and shows only a weak response to medication. Impulsive behaviors, both in and out of therapy, are highly disruptive. Intimate relationships are often chaotic, and this pattern can repeat itself in treatment, disrupting the therapeutic alliance. Cognitive symptoms also present problems for management.

What You Will Learn in This Book:

- Treatment For Extreme Borderline Personality Disorder
- Signs of Borderline Personality Disorder
- Borderline Personality Disorder Test
- Dealing With Clients With Borderline Personality Disorder

Chapter I

Borderline Personality Disorder

Borderline Personality Disorder (BPD) is a personality disorder in which the person displays a disrupted style and it usually affects people above the age of 18 years old. An individual with this disorder can have unstable moods of abnormal levels.

There's a tendency to view people in extreme conditions of possibly good or bad. They often idealize or maybe devaluate anyone who they meet up with. Without proper care and therapy, Borderline Personality Disorder can cause misfortune to an individual's relationships, at the office and with family members. Unstable social interactions, identity, self-image and habits are as well obvious in people affected by BPD.

Individuals with BPD are really hypersensitive regarding the events taking place in the surroundings all-around them. These people go through intense fear of abandonment and frustration which is incorrect, and also for reasonable separations from family. They fear being lonely and constantly desire to be in the company of men and women they are attached to.

To avert this condition they take impulsive steps like suicidal efforts. They change their mind-set toward well wishers or enthusiasts by idealizing them to devaluing them. Their plans plus opinion regarding values, career, types of associates, sexual identity are not steady and changes with situations.

About 36 years ago, I had a classmate in pre-med whose mood could swing from friendliness to extreme outbursts of anger over trifle issues within a matter of hours. We labeled him queer and always dealt with him with caution. In our fifth year in the medical school, during our Psychiatry posting, while treating the topic of Bipolar diseases, we believed his problem must be Manic-Depressive Psychosis. With the benefit of what I know now, I believe he probably had Borderline Personality Disorder.

Diagnostic and Statistical Manual of Mental disorders [DSM-IV] lists Borderline Personality Disorder as a psychiatric diagnosis and defines it as a prolonged disturbance of personality function. Adolph Stern used the term in 1938 to describe it because it lies on the borderline between neurosis and psychosis.

It is a serious disorder of the mind that causes affected persons to nurse a paralyzing fear of being abandoned by a loved one. The affected person manifests a siege mentality that makes him/her exhibit a bewildering range of emotions from idealizations like great admiration and love to devaluation such as intense anger and dislike within a short span of time.

Such a person exhibits outbursts of rage that lead to verbal and physical abuse against others. They read meaning into little matters and personalize issues becoming so extremely sensitive that they cannot sustain family relationships or workplace relationships.

Borderline Personality Disorder is basically a disorder of emotion control. A woman suffering from this condition could make life unbearable for the husband for coming late from work for any reason because she believes he must be having an affair.

The instability of mood in Borderline Personality Disorder results in unstable behavior, poor self-image and a distorted identity, all of which lead to social isolation. The level of frustration can be so high that it leads to self-injury of all sorts, attempted suicides and successful suicides in some cases.

The extreme feeling of insecurity makes them want love and pushes them in to sexual promiscuity and substance abuse. Divorce rate is high for the few who get married and did not seek professional help because of their chronic inability to manage their emotions.

In the United States, about 2% of adults mostly females suffer from BPD and it is responsible for 20% of hospital psychiatric admissions. The causes of Borderline Personality Disorder like many other ailments have been attributed to environmental and genetic factors.

However, 40 to 70% report a history of sexual abuse by a non-care giver. Recent research findings have linked Borderline Personality Disorder to impaired regulation of the neural circuits that modulate emotions. Amygdala, a part of the brain is part of this neural circuit.

Onset of the illness may be at adolescence or young adulthood. Triggers for precipitating this disorder include traumatic events like violence of all sorts, rape, alcoholism and substance abuse.

The outlook for this condition is good because it is amenable to proper mental health care and persons suffering from it can lead productive normal lives with appropriate care.

Symptoms may persist for years, but majority of symptoms decrease in severity over the years with some persons recovering fully from it. Therapy ranges from individual and group psychotherapy to

Dialectical Behavior Therapy, a new psychosocial therapy developed specifically for Borderline Personality Disorder.

Antidepressants and mood stabilizers are effective as symptomatic treatments for sufferers of this condition.

What you Need to Know About Borderline Personality Disorder

Do you think you might have borderline personality disorder or BPD? Well, you might have personality traits commonly exhibited by people with the disorder, but it doesn't necessarily mean that you have it. BPD, just like other personality disorders, involves a consistent pattern of thought and interaction between the person with the disorder and with his environment.

This pattern usually causes several problems and can impair the sufferer's ability take of himself or cope with life. The pattern for borderline personality disorder is usually characterized by unstable views about one's self, behavior, feelings and ability to interact with others, all of which can interfere with the person's ability to function normally.

In the past, BPD has been regarded as a set of signs and symptoms that include both psychosis (reality distortion) and neuroses (mood problems). People saw it as a condition that sits borderline between schizophrenia and mood problems. However, it has now been established that the condition is more similar to personality disorders, especially with the way it develops and occurs within families.

The actual causes of borderline personality disorder are still unknown, but there are family, genetic and social factors that are associated with its incidence.

The risk factors for the disorder are:

1. disrupted family life

2. poor family communication

3. abandonment during childhood and/or adolescence

4. sexual abuse. It occurs both in men and women, but mostly in women who are also receiving mental-health treatment. It affects about 6% of adults, and that is why it helps to know about the condition.

Borderline personality disorder has different symptoms. Most people with the disorder are unsure about themselves and their identity, thus their values and interests often rapidly change. They also frequently experience frequent changes in feelings or mood, and these often lead to unstable and intense relationships.

They also tend to view things in extremes, as if the world is in black and white. For example, if one thing isn't all good, then it must be all bad. Other symptoms include an irrational fear of abandonment and unwillingness to be alone. They often feel empty or bored when they are alone and are impulsive with their money and sexual relationships.

This impulsiveness can even lead to substance abuse, binge eating and shoplifting. They may also have frequent bouts of inappropriate anger and episodes of self-injury. If you exhibit some of these symptoms, you should consider a check up, especially if the symptoms are starting to or are already interfering with your daily life.

Like all the other personality disorders, borderline personality disorder is diagnosed based on a psychological examination. The history and severity of the symptoms are also being evaluated.

The good news is that BPD can be managed and treated. Many form of talk therapy are successful. These include dialectical behavioral therapy (DBT) and group therapy.

Medications can also help with the person's mood swing and to treat other conditions that can occur with BPD. Generally, the outlook will depend on the severity of the symptoms and on the person's willingness to accept help.

Chapter II

Borderline Personality Disorder Test

Borderline Personality Disorder known as BPD is a type of mental illness which is considered to be quite serious. It is characterized by instability in behavior, moods, interpersonal relations and self-image. Family and work life, long term planning and awareness of one's individual identity is usually affected by this instability.

Though this disorder is not as popular as bipolar disorder or schizophrenia, it does affect 2 percent of the adult population, mainly young women. The rate of self-harm without having the intention of suicide is high in such cases. In some cases patients suffering from Borderline Personality Disorder also tend to commit suicide. Over time many improve with help and are able to lead useful lives eventually.

While people suffering from bipolar disorder or depression tend to display continued state of mood for a longer period, people suffering from BPD may undergo severe outbreaks of anger, anxiety and depression lasting for a few hours or maximum a day. These may have associations with series of aggression which is impulsive, such as alcohol or drug abuse and injury to self.

Lack of self esteem is also common amongst patients suffering from BPD. They may feel mistreated unfairly, empty, or even bored at times. These symptoms are most severe when people having Borderline Personality Disorder feel that they do not have social support and are isolated.

The social relationships of people having BPD have highly unstable patterns. There is a change in their attitude towards their friends, family and loved ones, from love and great admiration to dislike and intense anger.

BPD often appears with other psychiatric problems such as bipolar disorder, anxiety disorders, depression, substance abuse, and other disorders. BPD is caused by the abnormal functioning of the Lymbic area of the brain controlling emotions.

A borderline personality disorder test is an evaluation used for diagnosing borderline personality disorder. A mental health professional administers the borderline personality disorder test. The test usually comprises of a series of questions or statements which the patient has to answer accordingly. If five or more symptoms are identified through the patient's answers then the diagnosis follow accordingly.

Some of the questions covered in the test are to check for reactions to abandonment, relationship issues, instability, self esteem, self image, self destructive behavior, suicidal thoughts, questions pertaining to feelings, especially feelings of emptiness and difficulty in controlling emotions, especially anger and ones revolving around paranoia and loss of reality.

There are a number of websites having border personality disorder test which can help you determine whether someone you care about may have the symptoms of BPD. Once you have administered the test you can then discuss the results with a mental health professional to help with diagnosis and treatment of BPD. The causes, symptoms, signs are generally covered by the borderline personality disorder test. Treatment along with the steps you can take by yourself to fight this condition should be recommended by qualified doctors only.

There have been improvements in the treatments for BPD in the past few years. Individual and group psychotherapy have produced positive results for many patients. A new treatment termed dialectical behavior therapy known as DBT, is a psychosocial treatment that is usually recommended for BPD and seems to be promising. Depending on the specific symptoms the patient has, medications may be prescribed.

Chapter III

Signs of Borderline Personality Disorder

What would happen if children at risk to develop Borderline Personality Disorder were able to get help in a early stage of its development? Most people do not know the characteristics of BPD and would be hard pressed to identify it in young children. Most people are helped when the mental health problem is full blown. In early adulthood, the symptoms scream for attention and become full blown.

There is the context out of which the BPD develops. Children from abusive families, emotionally, not just physically, are prone to develop the disorder. What is happening at home?

- emotionally cold parenting
- not able to express feelings
- black and white thinking: this is good; this is bad.
- crying episodes, seemingly without reason.
- daydreaming to excess. Starring
- observer rather than a participant to the extreme.
- sadness.
- facial expression that seems wooden, lack of smiling, even when happy.
- alcoholism in one or both of parents.
- siblings that are distant to each other.
- over achieving together with the other attributes.
- no rewards seem to change their poor self image. The self image is poor regardless of grades or achievements.

- older parents.
- parents that are overachievers
- reading and rereading questions to make sure they are "correct". Fear of failure.
- emotional numbness. Little emotional expression or self awareness. Face is like a mask.
- excessively "good", well mannered or the opposite.
- Unable to verbalize much about their family. Difficulty talking about their family specifically.
- small outbursts of opinion to galvanize a crowd. Easy prey for religious convention and cultism

People suffering from BPD have trouble moderating their emotions. Emotions come boiling to the surface in extremes. Moderating the emotional reactions seems beyond control.

When a child comes from an emotionally abusive family, this child might not be able to express anger at home without fear of punishment.

The anger becomes rage and goes underground. After stuffing the feelings so much, the child tries to turn off the feelings entirely so as not to be overwhelmed by these foreign and inconvenient feelings. Eventually, it becomes self numbing.

The other side is hysteria or emotional discharge to extremes, such as verbal explosions, or sobbing without seeming reason. The child is probably not aware of the reasons for the repression of ongoing family trauma.

To survive in the family, the child represses the memories to make it through.

In one case the child was caught between the parents on most every issue. Would you choose mother's side or father's side? Instead they were ground up in the middle of endless battles between parents.

There is no way to find an answer that does not upset one or the other parent? The personal interactions with primary caretakers becomes intensely painful. Later it is harder to choose side in an argument and to defend it without a feeling you will be annihilated or demolished. One teacher observed the child seemed to not like small talk.

The child does not know what he/she thinks, so small talk is painful. The child ego or center is trying to survive the daily barrage of attacks of parents and possibly siblings. If other children observe the parent's attacks, what is to prevents the siblings from being aggressive or hurtful. In there families, none of the children are getting their needs met.

Among siblings, it is natural to have rivalries and competition that reflect underlying deprivation that all the children are feeling. The children can feel jealousy toward the youngest, for example, but be unaware of why they are jealous. This type of dysfunctional family is very difficult to repair.

Family group psychiatric intervention is possible if the members are willing to work to improve their family. It is difficult to enrich these families where the parents are so invested in the dysfunction.

To try to give emotional support to the children is desirable to modify the damage of the family setting. There has to a place to go such as camp, Boys and Girls Club, or YWCA or other activities. The more the child spend time outside of the family, the more experiences they will have to compare to the original family situation. The experiences with normalcy, whether dinners at friends homes, sleep overs, and other activities, the greater the chance that the child will be able to refer back to these places for reference rather than the traumatic events of the home. BPD is a distorted reaction to living.

BPD persons frequently spend time alone. If the verbal interactions at home stimulate pain, why seek further conversations. Being quiet is a safe place. Eventually, the position of being stuck between to parents is a no win place to be.

Anxiety arises as the child anticipates future interactions. The child may develop a desire to please others. Trying to duck and stay out of the range of fire, whether it be debates or conversations is where you put your views on the line.

The BPD child will learn to hide their feelings. Being so afraid of attack on their very identity, why not invent some personalities or personna that are safe from attack. One personna might be the "good girl" or the funny kid or the empathetic observer.

Within these destructive homes, a BPD can read the atmosphere of their parents even before words are spoken. The antenna are out all the time. The only problem arises is that in the outside world not every one acts like your parents.

It is difficult to differentiate from an attack and a benign approach. These children need friends who have healthy households that they visit and get some healthy parenting. These friends homes are life saving.

The context of the family might show up in parent conferences and are one of the best indicators of potential BPD development. It occurs in some of the "nicest" families. The rigidity of their views might show something of the underlying events.

If the parents seem to need the child to be a trophy for their egos, that could be an indicator. These parents treat their children as objects to satisfy their own ego needs, so the achievement of the kids are bragged about by these parents. They are unable to see their children as rounded or with strengths and shortcomings.

Chapter IV

Symptoms of Borderline Personality Disorder

Is Borderline Personality Disorder affecting your private and professional life? Do you want to know more about the most frequent Symptoms associated with BPD?

Read on to unveil the nine most common manifestations of BPD!

1. Most common feature of Borderline Personality Disorder is the fear of abandonment and punishment. These phobias have their roots in childhood or teenage years and stem from negative parent-child relationships characterized by abuse, coldness, rejection, or inconsistent parenting. If divorce comes along with these negative parenting styles, the possibility in the child to develop borderline personality in the young adult years becomes important.

2. This abandonment fear leads to frequent anger and fury episodes. Real or imaginary signs of rejection, disrespect, or maltreatment coming from others are interpreted as signs of abandonment through the lens of past experiences in the home environment.

3. The third most common symptoms in borderline personality are the rapid mood changes. These do not have to lead to anger outbursts with every occasion, however they are difficult to manage and control, thus making one to run into challenges in the everyday activities.

4. The fourth most common sign of borderline personality is the chronic sense of internal void. Some sufferers describe it very well

as emotional or inner numbness. If left untreated this emotional state becomes stable and constant as a defensive response to the inner pain, anger, and distress.

5. The fifth most common sign of borderline personality is the destructive or potentially destructive behaviors toward the oneself. Such behaviors can be compulsive shopping, sex, substance abuse like alcohol and drugs, or binge eating.

6. The sixth specific symptom in borderline personality is comprised by the impulsive behaviors or decisions. These are made without too much weighing and usually without considering the repercussions. Such behaviors may be sudden leaves from relationships, job resignation, or school abandonment and are followed by feelings of remorse or regrets.

7. BPD individuals are also facing chaotic relationship mainly as a consequence of the abandonment dread. At the smallest hints or cues, reactions of anger and fury are triggered which occasionally will deliver the very thing a BPD sufferer fears, the abandonment.

8. Unhealthy and unadaptive self-perceptions are also frequently found in borderline personality since they emerge in the first years of life. When love, understanding, affection, and bonding are missing in the parent-child relationship, these unhelpful and critique types of self-perceptions will come along.

9. Also as a consequence of the unsupported home environment, young adults will have a tendency to recurrently look back into their past. This tendency stems from a self-protecting mechanism of the brain which frequently reiterates past memories in order to protect

the individual from present challenges. However this strategy reinforces the past fears instead of providing a real solution.

Ideas For Addressing Avoidant Borderline Personality Disorder

Are you struggling with Avoidant symptoms from Borderline Personality Disorder or BPD?

This avoidance stems from the powerful fear BPD sufferers feel from the perception of being abandoned or punished by others. These symptoms usually come together with negative self-attitudes which get triggered in certain circumstances.

Such self-attitudes and perceptions can lead one to an array of emotions like anxiety, shame, or anger. Such a strategy could bear quick results in the short run, however it will usually dial up the fear and angry reaction afterwards, spinning one into a vicious cycle.

Thus you need to adopt new strategies which can render long-term results in order to ease on your avoidant tendency and borderline personality.

The first strategy you should try out is to face your fears with the next occasion because this is going to help you to come up with new ways of perceiving reality. In such situations our brain triggers an in-built mechanism called habituation which helps us get used with previously fearfully perceived stimuli.

Next, try to stop the manifestations of your emotions and just watch closely how things evolve. This could be challenging at the beginning since you were used to act instantly on your emotions, however you should really try this out since it has the potential of betterment for you. Consequently ask yourself if the fear you are feeling is based on reality or not? In other words, are you having realistic reasons to be afraid of being abandoned?

If you will find this step difficult, try to think for a moment what would your life be without this fear? How much happier will your life and your relationships be if you could liberate yourself from this anguish and anxiety? Take in your hands the destiny of your life and be your boss, not your own emotional slave!

The second strategy you can try in order to overcome the BPB is to find new ways of seeing the world instead of the black and white pattern. It might be true that this thinking style was induced to you by your parents or entourage. Whatever the case, try to remember that the world we live in is rarely only black and white, and most of the times it has a lot of "gray" shadows in it.

Look to persevere in your endeavor because your short and long term benefits will exceed by far your present struggle and anger.

The third strategy you should implement in your daily life is comprised by the breathing exercises combined with meditation. This exercise liberates all the stress and tension accumulated during the day, helping you to relax and calm down your mind and body.

You will also discover hidden powers and energies within you to help you through the daily challenges. Also a calm and relaxed mind is significantly less prone to think in black and white only and is more opened to search for new ways of seeing and perceiving the world around.

Try doing this exercise at least once a day and, if done correctly, you should see improvements from day one in your quest to overcome borderline personality disorder.

Chapter V

Dealing With Clients With Borderline Personality Disorder

Clients with Borderline Personality Disorder need therapists to be good at listening, to be good at containing, to be good at setting boundaries, to be good at coping with very strong feelings, and to be good at working with complex transference and counter-transference issues. They also need you to have a great deal of patience.

There are various ways of understanding the Borderline Personality Disorder. Very few people today would still go with the historical psychoanalytic perspective which is that the Borderline Personality is on the borderline between psychosis and neurosis.

In other words, this kind of personality demonstrates many neurotic features and, under stress, slips into psychosis. In fact, most of those with a Borderline Personality Disorder do not go psychotic under stress and this is why we sometimes refer to them as being 'stably unstable.' They just stay predictably unstable in their self-image, in their mood, in their view of others, and so on.

The various more modern understandings of Borderline Personality Disorder emphasise different aspects of the problem. Most point to profound disturbances in the early mother-child relationship such that it leaves the person very damaged in terms of their relationships.

I think that this aspect is fundamental. So, what happens is that part of the person is stuck emotionally at the stage of being a baby, so in that part they easily feel empty because they did not get enough of the reliable attention, closeness, warmth, and unconditional acceptance.

So, what happens later on is that they are left with this tremendous neediness for this reliable closeness, warmth, and unconditional acknowledgement and acceptance and this becomes particularly obvious in their close relationships.

If the need is there and the person's partner is around, then the person will try to get the need met by the partner. So, they will want to be acknowledged, or held or listened to or made love to or whatever it is that will fill the hole.

If the need is not met, then tremendous rage can ensue and anyone who has been in a relationship with someone with this difficulty will be able to tell you about this rage. It is like the rage of Kali (you know the Indian goddess who is black and who wears a garland of human heads).

And when this rage comes out, one has one's head taken off in one way or another. To the person with the problem, they will usually experience it as being absolutely legitimate. The kind of response might be "All I asked for was acknowledgement, I don't think that was too much to ask"

It is often the case that the request was not such an unreasonable one. It's not unreasonable to ask for acknowledgement from one's partner, for example. Rather, it is the reaction to the request not being met that is so out of proportion for an adult. If the person was six weeks old and his or her needs were not being met, he or she would feel extremely distressed and this is what happens to six week old babies - they cry like hell if they are not happy.

People with a borderline disposition also feel tremendous distress if their deep-seated needs are not being met and because a very young part of themselves is being evoked. Consequently, if you are their partner and you are not meeting their needs, they may (and often do) feel betrayed by you and it is out of this sense of betrayal that the rage emerges.

Now the picture I have painted is a bit of a distortion in the sense that the infant part of the person with a Borderline Personality Disorder is not the only part of that person. There are child, adolescent and adult parts too.

In many cases, the adult parts realize the unreasonable their degree of emotions are, and they also realize how needy the neediness is and so they try to mask it.

It is only when the person is overwhelmed with neediness or rage or some other very strong infantile feeling that they can't help but let those aspects out. At those times they become adult sized infants from an emotional point of view and they can hate themselves for it afterwards when they have time to reflect on it.

In people with Borderline Personality Disorders, the infantile aspects may be present to greater or lesser extents. The greater the degree to which they are present, the greater is the borderline pathology. If they are in love with you, that love can be enormous and wonderful, but if they are disappointed in you, the disappointment can be shattering. So, they live in a world of great opposites and, from a psychoanalytic point of view, one of their main defences is splitting. So, everything is either wonderful or terrible and there tends to be very little middle ground, few shades of grey.

This is often apparent in their thinking too. They will tend to assess, say a friend as being either wonderful or awful and not as having some good points and some bad (as all of us do in reality). Cognitive therapists call this dichotomous thinking or black and white thinking.

The dichotomy applies in all realms and so it applies also to their sense of self. They tend either to be inflated: "The work I do is really special" or they tend to crash into a deflation: "I really am a useless piece of crap."

In their view of other people, the same splitting applies. They tend to see important others as being really wonderful or special or incredible and, when they become disappointed the person swings to a very negative position in their view and becomes completely untrustworthy, a total crap, and so on.

Consequently, in a relationship with someone with this pathology, you are on a roller-coaster ride. One minute you're useless and being criticized for everything and then you have to defend yourself. And, if through heated debate, your partner realizes that fault lies also with him or her, then they will try to crash into feelings of shame.

Remember, as a therapist, you're dealing with the same object relations. At the beginning of a therapy situation, someone with a Borderline Personality Disorder will only stick around if they have put you on a pedestal. An acceptable therapist is not an emotional possibility - you have to be special. Of course, the rule is that if you've been put on a pedestal, at some stage you have to fall off.

In fact, negotiating that falling off is a very important part of the therapy because it allows the person to learn to deal with the reality of shades of grey.

At the start of the therapy, however, they will need you to be special in the way that a mother should be special for a young baby. They need you to be there for them, they need you to be loving, they need you to be reliable, and they need you to listen very carefully to their experiences and their needs.

This careful listening is one of the most important aspects of all. If in doubt, just listen and reflect back their experience to them. That task, of course, is called mirroring by psychologists - and is one of the main tasks of mothers with infants. The infants get to know they exist and who they are by having themselves reflected back to themselves.

Remember, unconsciously, people with a Borderline Personality Disorder need the 'boundarylessness' of the early mother-child relationship and so by being convinced that you understand them profoundly, it becomes a situation for them where they think they are inside you.

Of course, the needs of the borderline client make limits of the therapy situation very difficult for both you and the client. They want to know that you really care and so, it is often the case, that they will want to meet up outside of the therapy situation. It is also hard for them to accept that there are limits on the therapy time and restrictions in terms of contact with you outside of this time. None the less, these limits are very important both for you and your client.

Now, one of the most difficult feelings for those with this disorder is that of abandonment. It feels to them as if they have lost all life in themselves - that they have died inside and been cast into this dark nightmarish world of an abandonment depression.

In dreams it emerges as death, dismemberment, darkness, and so on. Having a Borderline Personality Disorder in general is not easy. Everything feels unstable and is unstable. Part of the reason is that part of the personality is very young and very damaged.

Another reason is that the personality has not yet fused properly. In normal personality development, somewhere between two and six, we integrate a view of ourselves and the world as part of what Jungian analysts call the ego. And so we believe ourselves to be particular kinds of people - 'I'm a good little girl and I like to be helpful' or 'I'm a bit of a naughty girl and I like to have lots of fun' and so on. Our awareness of the aspects of ourselves that we don't like then slips into what Jung called the shadow. This is a healthy process.

In the case of those who are developing a Borderline Personality Disorder, this integration doesn't take place. So what happens is that the person keeps on slipping between the dominance of one complex and another. One minute, they may feel proud of their work and then they may get an indication that they have made a mistake and they may then flip into a state in which they are dominated by another complex in which they feel like the greatest failure that ever walked upon the earth.

This instability is usually reflected in all aspects of their being. For example, people with Borderline Personalities are often uncertain as to what it is that they want to do with their lives. Part of the problem is that different parts of themselves may want different things.

One part may need to be creative, another may need security, another may be primarily interested in power and a fourth may have spiritual interest that clashes with all the rest.

To compound it all, any of the parts can predominate at any time. So, for example, the part that is interested in spirituality may want to go on a retreat and get excited about it and book it and then, as it approaches, the part that is fearful of abandonment may dread the thought of going off on her own.

These shifts around the personality can take place hundreds of times a day and so it is difficult living the life of someone with this disorder.

There is also a remarkable incidence of sexual abuse in the background of these people and many think that repeated traumas (including sexual abuse) are part of the cause of the disorder.

I think that, in the case of many girls, it works like this. As an infant they did not have their needs met for a reliable, loving, unconditionally accepting mother. This left them with a life-long need to find this good mothering.

In trying to find it as a child they may approach men who are very damaged in their own sexuality and who find the closeness and trust they can establish with them sexually exciting. These men then exploit the girl's need for love by satisfying their sexual needs with them. Part of the little girl is so desperate for this love that she goes along with it all but another part of them knows this is not OK and is traumatised by it all. People who have had this kind of experience as children tend to confuse sexuality and love and so as teenagers and adults, tend to try to get their needs for maternal love met through sexual relationships which often doesn't work.

Of course, there are many more horrific scenarios than this where the child's desperate need for love leads them into situations where they are much more severely abused. If the abuse is very extreme, them Multiple Personality Disorder, rather than Borderline Personality Disorder will probably be the result.

Another historical factor for those with a Borderline Personality Disorder is that, because their ego was so fragile and their feelings so strong, many experiences which might not traumatize others might have devastated someone who is on the way to developing a Borderline Personality Disorder.

Take as an example, a boy of four who had poor early mothering (with many abandonment experiences) and look at the situation where he was taken to school for the first time and left there by his mother. Now, many children find this difficult but most cope (and the incident doesn't get left as a trauma).

What would tend to happen for our little boy is that he would have a catastrophic abandonment reaction and the incident would generate such strong feelings that he would be overwhelmed and the incident would then remain as part of a series of memories of traumatic abandonments. In many ways such a child would build up a whole library of traumatic memories - of abandonments, of betrayals, and of various abuses. Many, or all of these experiences may be the kinds of experiences we all go through - like going to school, like losing friends, like moving to a new home, like having someone con us and so on.

To our budding borderline personality, however, their emotional reaction to these events overwhelms their fragile egos and leaves further traumatic memories.

As I said, it is not easy to have a Borderline Personality Disorder and they experience themselves often as people who struggle in life. Often this struggle comes up in their dreams. There will be a symbol of things coming together - like a dream of a marriage and then there will be dreams of things falling apart again - divorces, disintegration, and so on.

And, this is how it goes - struggling to get it together and then it all falls to pieces again.

People with a Borderline Personality Disorder also tend to carry a tremendous lot of shame that emerged out of their experiencing of not being loved.

Because the degree of shame is great and because their ego is fragile, they tend to avoid shame at all costs because to experience it has catastrophic results.

So, for example, if something went wrong ,they would tend to protect themselves from the shame by tending to blame others and this can be a very annoying aspect of living with someone with a Borderline Personality Disorder.

ay you are married to someone with such a problem. You will, at times, get stuck in the position of either having to accept unjust blame or having to go through the battle to get the blame back where it belongs with all the consequences that ensue because, if your partner then accepts the blame then he or she will probably collapse into a part of themselves that has an extremely negative view of themselves. and they will be subdued by shame and their mood may drop considerably as a result and so they may be depressed for days. This process is hard for both people involved.

A related problem occurs in therapy with those with a Borderline Personality. Sooner or later in the therapy, you are going to 'screw up' in their eyes and this is going to produce strong negative feelings, disappointment, anger, and so on.

The thing to do in this situation is to listen carefully and reflect without getting defensive in any way even if you think that whatever you did was reasonable.

Later on, when the crisis in the relationship has passed, then the incident can be worked through so that it can be understood in a more reasonable light.

So, as an example, you may forget an appointment. It happens sometimes. Your client may feel abandoned and enraged as a result. If you listen to their feelings and apologise, then it will usually turn out OK.

On the other hand, if you become defensive and say that you're only human and that you think their reaction is totally out of proportion and so on, then they will remain stuck in the conviction that you have done some terribly wrong and, if there have been other aspects of their experience of you which they didn't like, an official complaint may be the next step or they may even sue you.

The deep seated motivation behind this would be the desire to see you hurt as much as they are hurting - as they see it - as a result of your actions. I would guess that the majority of official complaints against therapists come from those with Borderline Personality Disorders.

To prevent this, in the vast majority of situations, all you have to do is hear the person out and apologize.

I think that the core aspect of the treatment of people with this difficulty is to have them have an experience of unconditional love and acceptance and you need to aim for this for at least the first year or two of the therapy so that they can have a corrective emotional experience.

As they come to feel accepted and cared for, so they themselves will begin to question their reactions and this will open up the possibilities for honest discussion of the objective situation and that is the time to begin to see their reactions more realistically.

They can do it then because the relationship between you and them bolsters the strength of their egos. The experience of being accepted and loved has to come first.

Over time in therapy, the continuing sense of being held, listened to, cared for and so on, allows for a gradual integration of the various aspects of the personality. This just happens as a natural part of the process. In other words, given that you have set adequate boundaries and have an attitude of care and spend a lot of energy on careful listening and reflecting, then the process of healing in the personality will unfold and, in this sense, you will be taught by your client as to how to do the work.

Remember, the unconditional positive regard is not the same thing as colluding with the regressed part of the personality. In other words, you can reflect back the person's emotional experience accurately without colluding with any distortion of reality.

A similar attitude needs to be taken towards their feelings towards you. They will see you in an inflated way and this has to be accepted as their perception of you. When you fall from grace, this has to be accepted as their perception too. As I said, over time, they will give you indicators that they are willing to take a more realistic look at their reactions and that is the time to do it.

Another of the defences used by those with Borderline Personality Disorders is projective identification. I'm sure that most of you are familiar with this defence but, for those who are not, I'll try and describe it.

Projective identification is a primitive defence used when the person can't cope with very strong feelings. What happens is that they then split these feelings and attitudes off and dump them to you.

All of this happens unconsciously. Don't ask me how, but it happens. So, for example, if they are feeling unconsciously that they are a miserable failure, you can come out of the session feeling like a miserable failure.

So something that you have to remind yourself of, time and time again, is that if you come out of a session full of negative attitudes or emotion, ask yourself if these attitudes and emotions more properly fit with your client. Once you have this insight, it helps to diffuse the experience but, if you don't have the insight, you can be sitting with these feelings for days.

Projective identification is an unpleasant experience as a recipient but it does give valuable clues as to what it is that you client is struggling to avoid in themselves.

The cognitive-behavioural therapists emphasise education as being an important part of the therapy and I think that there is some sense in this. What they recognise is that these people struggle not to get overwhelmed by their feelings.

They also have noticed that many of them have not learned how to cope with strong feelings and so they tend to act out their feelings or try to stop them in some potentially harmful way.

So, for example, if they get really angry, they may smash their fist which is not a particularly helpful way of dealing with anger. If they feel abandoned, they may threaten to commit suicide to try and win your concern back.

Again, this is not a very constructive strategy in the long run. If they feel unmanageable anger, they may cut themselves in order to dissipate the feeling. If they feel empty, they may binge-eat or shop excessively in order to try to fill themselves up.

If they feel unwanted, they may sleep around in order to try and feel loved and so on. If they have any feeling they don't want to have to cope with, they may get drunk or stoned to try and escape or may even take an overdose of medication like sleeping tablets. These are all destructive ways of dealing with feelings and you, as a therapist, can help them to learn to cope with these feelings in more constructive ways.

Chapter VI

Treatment For Extreme Borderline Personality Disorder

Borderline personality is commonly observed during adolescence, characterized by mood instability, self-image distrurbance and emotional liability. This ailment is expected to dissolve by maturity, with effective personality development. Though borderline personality disorder is not an incapacitating mental condition, like schizophrenia, it is considered a very serious illness by most psychiatrists because of the harm an afflicted person may bring upon him or her self, during the peak of stress.

About 75 percent of those diagnosed with borderline personality disorder exhibit self-mutilation, drug addiction, alcoholism and suicidal attempts. Out of this population who practice self destructive behaviors, about 8 to 10% actually die. These alarming results prompt medical experts to address the mental ailment with effective treatments.

The first line of treatment that is recommended is psychotherapy. This helps patients learn to control their emotions, take responsibility for their lives and use positive coping mechanisms to get through challenges.

Psychotherapy employs the "no-suicide" contract to lessen the possibility of deaths and at the same time, empower the patient to contradict his own despair and seek support when needed.

Psychotherapy also provides an avenue for cognitive restructuring, wherein a person's negative and faulty perception of him or her self and world is corrected.

For extreme cases, hospitalization is advised. Severe depression will drive a person with borderline personality disorder to commit suicide and succeed at it. To prevent this, constant supervision and immediate medical treatment is required.

Hospitals and psychiatric institutions have the necessary facilities to secure the individual's safety and health. These establishments also have adequate amounts of staff that could observe and attend to the needs of the patients, in a manner that would be most therapeutic for them.

In conjunction with psychotherapy and hospitalization, medication is given to control the destructive symptoms of borderline personality disorder and improve the person's well-being. Low doses of antipsychotic drugs are given to people with borderline personality disorder during brief psychotic episodes.

Antidepressants are prescribed for treatment of specific emotional states.

What Treatments are available?

There are three treatments that people suffering from Borderline Personality disorder can receive. There are talking treatments, therapeutic communities, and alternatives.

Talking treatments

Given that drugs are also prescribed during psychotherapy or talking therapies. These kinds of talks aim to find the roots of the feelings and behavior of the patient. In this case, the therapist also builds a relationship with the patient. This is seen as an important link to your past and present relationship. Being able to explore on this relationship is a helpful break to the unhealthy patterns of your relationships.

There are also some forms of counseling that are synonymous to psychotherapy, like psychodynamic counseling for example. This type of counseling places great emphasis on childhood experience, which could also be one of the causes of the disorder.

Cognitive behavior therapy on the other hand, is a short term treatment that is more focused on the everyday difficulties, and practicalities.

Therapeutic communities

There are some inpatient communities that specialize in treating personality disorders. In this type of therapeutic community, both staff and residents have to share the responsibility of tasks and decisions. Deciding to go into a therapeutic community means being ready to talk to your life about other members of the group. This could be especially hard, specially on the first treatments.

What's good about being part of the community is that you become aware of your concerns as well as others feelings towards yours and their actions. You can get a perspective of what its like being on the other person's shoes, and discover what you would like to change about yourself which leads to individual therapy and hopefully, medication.

Alternative therapies

Alternative therapies for borderline personality disorder are new discoveries which have been found to be helpful for alleviating some concerns and symptoms. Some of these therapies are yoga and acupuncture.

Chapter VII

Borderline Personality Disorder And Bipolar Disorder - How They Are Different

Borderline Personality Disorder is not as common as Bipolar, and also we know less about this illness. Twenty percent of hospital admissions for mental illness are diagnosed with this disorder, while fifty percent of hospitalizations for mental illness are bipolar patients. Young women group are more known to develop Borderline Personality Disorder, while bipolar affects both men and women equally regardless of age.

Mood swings such as anxiety, depression and violent flare ups are experienced in both patients with Borderline Personality Disorder and those with Bipolar. With Bipolar patients these symptoms can last weeks or months in a cycle, while in Borderline Personality Disorder it may only last a few hours or a day.

With Borderline Personality Disorder, a patient can reach periods where they they do not know what their likes and dislikes are, who they are as a person or their personal preferences. Their long term goals may change quite often, and trying to stick to one activity becomes difficult. They act on impulse with overeating, shopping sprees and may indulge in sexual liaisons with strangers. Mania is also present in bipolar patients.

Patients with Borderline Personality Disorder also experience emptiness, feelings of being misunderstood or mistreated and worthlessness; much like the symptoms felt in depression of patients with Bipolar.

In terms of relationships, a patient with Borderline Personality Disorder will have extremes of hating someone with a passion. One minute they will be in love, then a small conflict will instantly make them hate that person. If they fear being abandoned, the patient gets depressed, feels rejection and may threaten suicide. Bipolar patients also have these issues when it comes to relationships.

Treatments for both disorders are also similar. A psychiatrist will prescribe both medication and therapy, the preferred choice.

Cognitive Behavioural Therapy was originally developed in patients with Borderline Personality Disorder, but found to be successful for Bipolar patients. There are various medications for both mental illnesses which have been to achieve good results.

There is little known about both illnesses which are thought to be either genetic or due to the environment. Research shows that the nature of Bipolar is more biological and hereditary, whereas Borderline Personality Disorder is due more to the stimuli of the environment and situations.

These similarities show that either illness is difficult to distinguish and diagnose, for doctors and psychologists, too. Anyone who is suffering from these symptoms should medical or professional advice for the correct diagnosis and treatment.

Self diagnosis is not the best way to go about treating your symptoms especially with Bipolar and Borderline Personality Disorder. A psychiatrist or psychologist is the best person to advise you in order for successful treatment to be prescribed, and give you the best chance for managing your mental illness for a better future.

Chapter VIII

Borderline Personality Disorder and Rage

If you've been diagnosed with Borderline Personality Disorder, there is a good chance you have experienced more than your share of Borderline rage. What exactly is Borderline rage? It is intense anger that is directed outward toward another thing or person.

Sometimes it is directed inward and will manifest in self-abusing behaviour such as cutting. Most often Borderline rage is directed at the person you care most about, the person you want most to love you.

This sets up an almost endless tug of war between the person diagnosed with Borderline Personality Disorder and their loved ones. In some cases, Borderline rage can be directed at anyone in the room. Any convenient target, that is. These bouts of intense anger are quite often sparked by the person's desire to be close to their loved one but being afraid to trust them enough to allow them close enough to care and thus to reject them.

Where does it come from?

Borderline rage is rooted in abandonment issues usually from preverbal times in a child's life. Because the child has no language the hurt is deep and often inaccessible except through therapy.

Borderline rage will often come boiling to the surface in the most seeming of innocent exchanges. In my case, I could go from zero to nuclear in a matter of minutes when provoked. I, like most of the people who cared about me, was almost always taken by surprise because I simply did not know what caused it to bubble up and ignite into a frenzied explosion.

I learned in therapy that my rage was deeply seated in having been abandoned as a young baby (at only six months of age). It was further compounded by growing up with a father who had his own rage issues but never learned how to properly express his anger so it was bottled up deep inside him and would come spilling out at inappropriate times.

I firmly believe that people with Borderline Personality Disorder are made. They are not born that way.

Who can possibly love me?

People with Borderline Personality Disorder find it almost impossible to believe that someone can love them for who they are because, after all, they often do not have any sense of who they are to begin with.

When they find someone who says they love them, they will test them over and over again in order to get them to prove their love. In essence, they bite the hand that feeds them. They set the stage for the other person to abandon them and repeat the old pattern all over again in an almost never-ending cycle.

It can be very tricky to learn to be a different person. It starts with introspection. Introspection, which is done through therapy, leads to insight and insight enables change.

The person with Borderline Personality Therapy can learn to recognize their triggers and figure out new ways to respond to them. Respond as opposed to react. I used to say that I "had cancer in my soul" but after years and years of therapy that cancer is now in remission.

Some days I think it has been cured entirely but I know that is not the case. I have learned to manage and regulate my emotions but must be ever-vigilant so as not to slip back into old behavior patterns.

Conclusion

Borderline rage is driven by fear and anxiety

When you actually sit down and think about it, borderline rage is driven by fear and anxiety. Fear and anxiety about being abandoned by those we love. Fear and anxiety about being hurt again. Fear and anxiety about not being able to control one's own environment and the relationships in which we are engaged. When the person with Borderline Personality Disorder begins to learn, understand and believe through therapy that their own cognitive distortions about the nature of their relationships is what keeps them stuck in this endless cycle, they can begin to approach their relationships differently. They can learn to stop being angry and full of rage at the entire world at large and renegotiate their closest relationships so they can enjoy them.